Jesus and my Gender

By Dale Partridge

Illustrated by Brad Smith

Relearn Press
PRESCOTT, ARIZONA

© 2022 by Relearn.org. All rights reserved.

No portion of this book may be reproduced, stored in a retrieval system, or transmitted in any form or by any means— electronic, mechanical, photocopy, recording, scanning, or other—except for brief quotations in critical reviews or articles, without the prior written permission of the publisher.

Published in Prescott, Arizona by Relearn.org
Written by Dale Partridge
Illustrated by Brad Smith
First Edition / First Printing.
Printed in the U.S.A.

Scripture taken from the English Standard Version®. Copyright © 2008 by Crossway. Used by permission. All rights reserved.

Relearn Press is a companion ministry of Relearn.org. For information, please contact us through our website at Relearn.org.

"So God created man in his own image,
in the image of God he created him;
male and female he created them."

Genesis 1:27

A Vital Note for Parents & Guardians

This book would have been absurd to every generation before us. But we also know that sin is always on the move perverting and distorting God's design. It has become clear that this culture is playing for keeps, and they want the heart and mind of your child. For that reason, this book and books like it have become essential tools for wise Christian parents.

Years ago, a man once told me, "If you believe wrong, you will never live strong." As parents and guardians, it's our duty to train our children to believe rightly about everything from God and His Gospel to human gender, sexuality, and identity. That is the aim of this book. In today's culture, we should expect every child to witness some form of blatant gender or sexual distortion by the age of five. In fact, we should expect this to occur on a regular basis. As you know, the world is attempting to detach gender from sex and produce extra-biblical categories of personhood. These ideas are sinful and dangerous for humanity and must be aggressively rejected by the Church.

For that reason, we must establish our children in truth, so they can view these public perversions of gender and sexuality as sinful and abnormal expressions of human behavior.

However, in addition to the defensive work parents must perform to guard their children against these lies, there is also a great value in teaching children God's purpose and instruction for males and females. But it's not only important that boys know about the male gender and girls know about the female gender. Boys and girls must also learn about each other's God-given genders. Namely, a little boy doesn't only need a vision for what it means to become a godly man, but he also needs to know what it will mean for a girl to become a godly woman.

Now, this book is only one tool in your toolbox. Nevertheless, I believe the truths in this book delivered at the right time in a child's life, will make a big impact in maintaining a biblical view of themselves. I encourage you to commit to reading this book every day for five days straight, look up the Scripture references and read them aloud, have discussions with your child, and have them memorize the answers to the short kid's catechism on biblical gender located at the back of the book.

Keep fighting for the truth,

Dale Partridge

Founder of Relearn.org and Reformation Seminary

"Youth is susceptible to evil doctrine. Whether we teach young Christians truth or not, the devil will be sure to teach them error. They will hear of it, even if they are watched by the most careful guardians. The only way to keep chaff out of the child's little measure is to fill it brimful with good wheat. Oh, that the Spirit of God may help us to do this!"

Charles Spurgeon

Before the creation of the world,
God designed boys and girls.

Genesis 1:27; Matthew 19:4-5

He made the boys and called them male—
their strength and size will soon prevail.

Proverbs 20:29

But girls God made the glory of man,
their grace and beauty to serve His plan.

1 Corinthians 11:7

He called the girls female—
immaculate and pure—
for He designed them wonderf'lly,
that they should be secure.

Genesis 2:21-23; Psalm 139:14

The boys were just as awesome—fast and excellent—
for He designed them wonderf'lly, a perfect testament.

Proverbs 20:29; Psalm 139:14

Improvements were not needed,
for in God's image they each stood.

Genesis 1:31; Ephesians 2:10

There was no need for more; male and female were sufficient. To add to God's design is wrong and inconsistent.

Genesis 5:1–2; Mark 10:6

Some people like to say
that gender can be picked;
But this is foolish thinking;
for genders can't be switched.

Rom. 1:24-26; 1 Cor. 6:18; Eph. 4:17-24; Prov. 17:20, 6:12-15

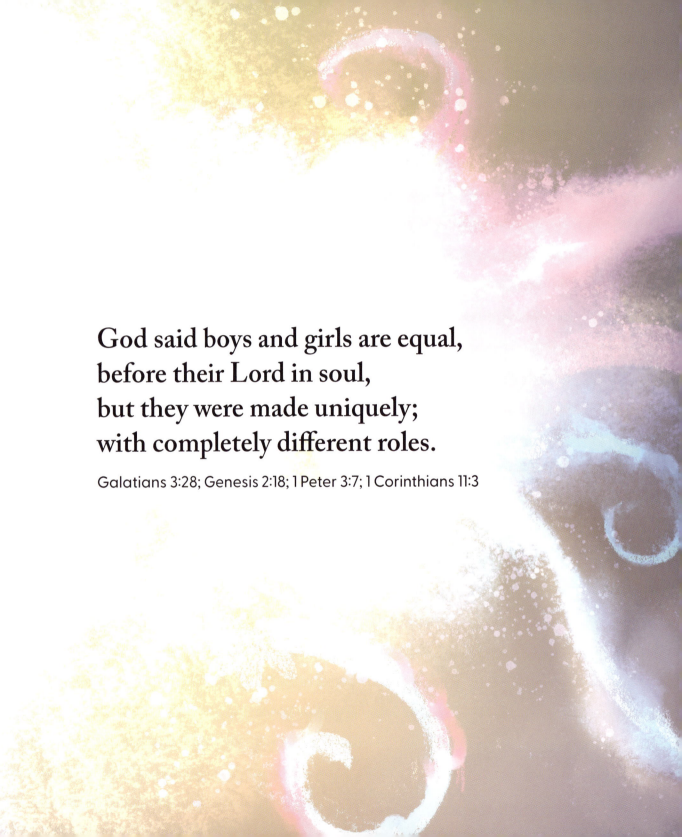

God said boys and girls are equal,
before their Lord in soul,
but they were made uniquely;
with completely different roles.

Galatians 3:28; Genesis 2:18; 1 Peter 3:7; 1 Corinthians 11:3

The boys were made to love, protect, and to provide.

Ephesians 5:24; Genesis 3:16; Ephesians 5:23; Colossians 3:18-19; 1 Timothy 5:8

His girls were called to help, to serve, and glorify.

Genesis 2:18; Titus 2:3-5; Proverbs 31:10-31

He built His boys for rough and play; just how they ought to be. They'd pounce and battle for the day; and even jump from trees!

2 Sam. 23:8–38; Ps. 144:1-2

He made them strong to guard their friends,
to protect the weak, and make amends.

Psalm 82:3-4; Isaiah 1:17; Matthew 5:9

Not only were they rough, but noble and hardworking.

Proverbs 21:5; 12:11; 13:4; 14:23

They know the truth's enough and fight for righteous living.
Matthew 5:6; 1 Timothy 6:12; Ephesians 6:10-18; Joshua 24:15

But most of all, they know their Lord;
Jesus Christ, their Savior.
He's the King of all their life
and deserves their best behavior.

Mark 12:29-30; John 14:15; James 1:22; Romans 12:1-2

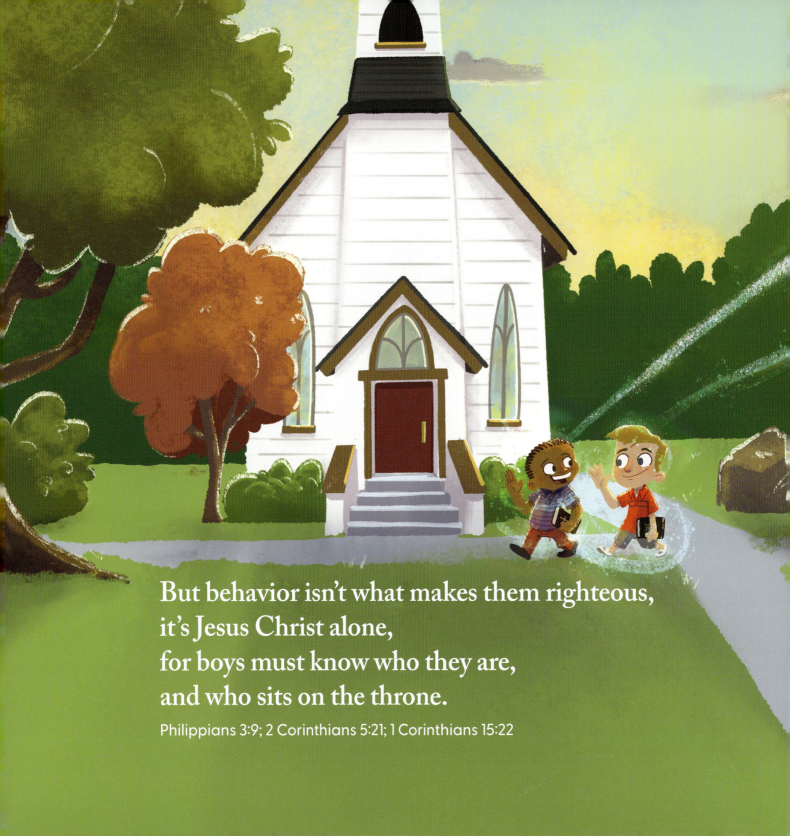

But behavior isn't what makes them righteous,
it's Jesus Christ alone,
for boys must know who they are,
and who sits on the throne.

Philippians 3:9; 2 Corinthians 5:21; 1 Corinthians 15:22

Jesus Christ, King of Kings,
Designer of their gender—
He's the One who made them male;
in that they rest forever.

1 Timothy 6:13-16; Revelation 19:16; Philippians 2:10-11

But what about the girls, the glory of mankind?
What did Jesus say of their design He had in mind?

Genesis 2:22–24; 1 Corinthians 11:7

When He made His girls, He formed them right,
with eloquence and love.
He gave them gentleness, a servant's heart,
and compassion from above.

Genesis 2:18; Proverbs 31:10-31; Psalm 139:13-14

The crown of girls is quickly seen when people start comparing— a special privilege given them: the blessing of childbearing.

1 Corinthians 11:12; John 16:21

The female body is extraordinary,
the boys cannot relate.
The girls can carry babies
and nurture those they make.

Psalm 127:3-5; 139:13; 22:9; Luke 11:27-28

Most of all, and like the boys,
the girls have a Lord,
The Son of God—Jesus Christ—
the King they must adore.

1 Samuel 2:1-10; Exodus 15:20-21; John 20:16-18

But boys and girls cannot miss
the greater purpose yet,
for God designed them intentionally
to make a perfect set.

One day in the future,
the boys will become men.
Their hearts will seek a girl
to marry 'til life ends.

Genesis 2:18, 2:24; Proverbs 18:22; Ephesians 5:33

The two that once were separate,
will become one in their Lord.
They will share a love together,
and a family to look toward.

The man will be the shepherd,
leading their family toward the truth.
The woman will keep closely,
helping her family love God, too.

Ephesians 5:22-32; Proverbs 22:6; Ephesians 6:4

So while boys and girls have different bodies,
roles, and unique functions,
They are the same before their Lord—
His design should be instructive.

We must remember God is perfect,
holy, and all wise.
He doesn't make mistakes,
and He never is surprised.

1 Corinthians 11:12; John 16:21; 1 Timothy 1:17

So, if you were born a boy, be excited and content.
You're a male for a reason, and your gender was God-sent.

Ephesians 2:10; Psalm 139:13-14

If you were born a girl, be thrilled, for you are marvelous! You're a female for a reason, and your value is no less.

Psalm 119:73, 71:6; Galatians 3:28

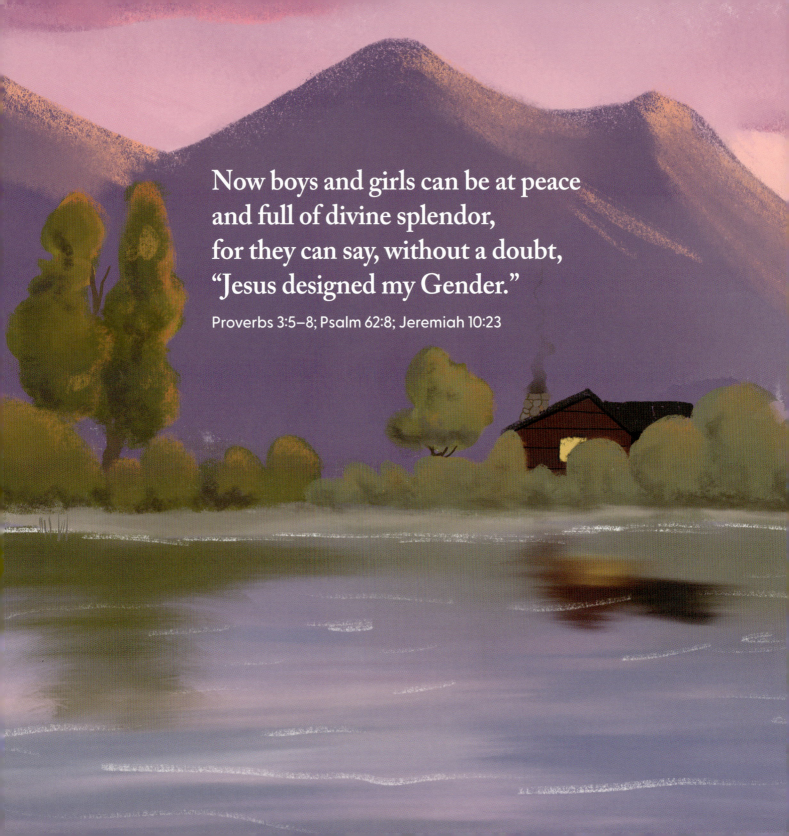

Now boys and girls can be at peace
and full of divine splendor,
for they can say, without a doubt,
"Jesus designed my Gender."

Proverbs 3:5–8; Psalm 62:8; Jeremiah 10:23

Five Questions & Answers for Kids!

Parents, read this book five days in a row. After each reading, help your child memorize the answers to each of the following questions.

Q1. Who is the Maker of boys and girls?
A: God is the Maker of boys and girls.

Q2. How many genders did God make?
A. God made only two genders: Male and Female.

Q3. Did God make you a male or female?
A. God made me a _____.

Q4. Are boys and girls the same?
A. No, boys and girls have equal value, but we have different bodies, roles, and functions.

Q5. How can you glorify God as a _____?
A. As a _____, I can glorify God by living out the Bible's instructions for my gender.